STOP THE TORMENT!

MATTHEW LOHR

xulon
PRESS

Copyright © 2013 by Matthew Lohr

Stop The Torment!

by Matthew Lohr

Printed in the United States of America

ISBN 9781626979369

All rights reserved solely by the author. The author guarantees all contents are original and do not infringe upon the legal rights of any other person or work. No part of this book may be reproduced in any form without the permission of the author. The views expressed in this book are not necessarily those of the publisher.

Unless otherwise indicated, Bible quotations are taken from the King James Version of the Bible.

www.xulonpress.com

You're probably not aware that you have been drinking poison while expecting someone else to suffer from it. That's a description of what it's like to hold a grudge, to have unforgiveness in your heart toward someone. Anger, along with resentment and bitterness, stirs a cocktail of torment that you've been drinking if you have unforgiveness in your heart. It's in your system, and you're the only person who can make the decision to dilute that tormenting poison.

Thank you for taking your time to read my book. I am aware of the value of time, and I am convinced that it will be time well spent. It has taken many hours of writing and editing this book so that I could simply and accurately pass along this vital information. I believe that you are reading this book because of a greater plan and purpose for your life; I do not believe in coincidence. It is up to you, however, what you do with the knowledge that you gain. Forgiving those who have harmed you or someone you love may seem radical, but I assure you, the relief is well worth the decision to forgive. I have learned that you must act on what you learn to get the results you want. I have personally received counseling from some of the best health-care professionals in the world, but until I acted on their instructions, absolutely nothing changed.

The intent of this book is to pass along biblical wisdom that I have learned over a lifetime. It will encourage you and quickly take you to a better place in life as you cooperate with these truths. I pray that you will have revelation knowledge given to you as you follow the biblical plan of forgiveness. I pray that if you have lost hope, your hope will be restored. It truly is up to you if you want things to change.

I can tell you what learning to quickly forgive has done for me. It has kept me at peace when others were freaking out, and I have learned that I have more control over my own life than I realized. I don't have to ride life's emotional roller coaster, because I choose to quickly forgive and relax instead of getting angry. I have also learned that when I hold a grudge, I'm allowing the one who hurt me to have control over that part of my life. Why would I want someone who has hurt me to have any influence over my life?

I hope that as you read and consider what's written in the following pages, you will see that it's for your benefit to forgive. When I was an army medic, I learned that when someone is sick or wounded, they need proficient and immediate care, and that is why I have purposefully kept this book short and to the point. This book was written for you and for those in your life who need you to be a better you. The information in it will help you unlock things that have kept you bound and then release healing into those wounds that were caused by others.

It is possible that you may need to forgive someone who hurt you many years ago, though you rarely think about it. It is also possible that you need to forgive someone who caused pain that still haunts you; it's like an open wound, and you just can't seem to get it out of your mind. I want you to keep in mind that choosing to forgive is for your benefit, and it has nothing to do with justifying anyone who has hurt you. Forgiveness awards emotional and physical healing that you cannot receive any other way. Forgiveness is like a master key that unlocks rivers of healing, peace, and joy into your life. When you choose to forgive, you are choosing a better life—for you and for the people you love.

Naturally, we resist remembering past painful events; we typically bury them or lock them away in the vaults of our minds and then hang a sign on the vault door that says, "Do Not Enter." I have heard it said many times, "Forgive and forget." But unless you come down with amnesia, your mind will never forget. However, it is possible to remove the pain of those negative memories and even replace them with compassion towards the person or people who hurt you. Oh, now you think I have completely lost my mind, but I'm telling you from my own life experience that with God all things truly are possible. It is possible to be moved with compassion after you begin to understand some things.

The door by which emotional pain entered your life may also be the same door for it to leave. You may have to remember some things you would rather not think about, but keep in mind it is temporary discomfort on the way to a better life. When I was a medic, splinting a fracture or starting an IV would initially cause discomfort, but the end result was always worth the temporary pain. I have learned that many times the path to healing will be temporarily uncomfortable. I am convinced that all wounds must specifically be addressed for them to properly heal. I will explain this in greater detail a little later.

Many times emotional wounds are inflicted during childhood. We are told that names and what others say mean nothing, yet they have influenced all of us to some extent. Remember this little rhyme: "Sticks and stones may break my bones, but names will never hurt me"? Perhaps you even sang it, but those names did hurt, and they left a painful sting even to this day. Words are very powerful; in fact, the Bible says that words carry life or death. "Death and life are in the power of the tongue: and they that love it shall eat the fruit thereof" (Prov. 18:21).

Mean things that have rolled off the tongues of other children may have opened doors of resentment and bitterness into your life. Children have been known to say some very hurtful things. They probably were repeating things they heard and maybe even things said to them by adults who should know better. Many times we say things without thinking them through; we have all probably done that at some point in our lives.

Perhaps the hard things you faced as a child have motivated you to succeed in life. Maybe you grew up poor or were told you would never amount to anything, but now after years of hard work, you have obtained some success. It is also possible that things said to you have paralyzed you, and now you're afraid to try anything outside your comfort zone because inwardly you believe the negative words that someone said.

Many adults are still subconsciously working to receive acceptance from a father or mother who was impossible to please. Maybe you have failed in some area of life, and now that just seems to confirm that what they said was true. Failure is part of the process; how you handle fear is up to you. You may choose to throw your hands up and say, "I tried, but they were right." On the other hand, you could say, "If at first you don't succeed, try and try again." Many well-known people who have changed the course of history experienced failure; some of them failed hundreds of times. Thomas Edison said he didn't fail a thousand times, but just figured out a thousand ways not to make a lightbulb.

The apostle Paul (who was first Saul), in his zealousness to keep God's law, persecuted the first followers of Jesus and was even an accomplice in the murder of Stephen the evangelist. Abraham Lincoln had a public nervous breakdown; he also failed in business and lost some elections, but then he became president of the United States and abolished slavery. If you choose a lifestyle of being slow to anger and quick to forgive, then your energy and focus can be on the most important matters, and you may very well change the course of history. In fact, I am sure that you can improve or even change the course of your life and leave a positive mark on your world.

It is vital that you have positive focus in life because focusing on bad memories has ruined too many relationships, including many marriages. That is why it is imperative to confront and extinguish subconscious negative, destructive thoughts, feelings, and memories once and for all. Those words spoken that have set destructive paths in your life can and will be extinguished by acting on the biblical knowledge that you gain from this book. Anger, resentment, and bitterness are a trio of destructive behaviors that must be stopped, not only for you, but for the people you love and those who love you.

Now I want you to keep in mind that as you remember some of these negative things that happened in your life, it is not for the purpose of joining the "poor me" club, but instead that you can become a lifetime member in the "I am free" club. In other words, don't allow yourself to be influenced anymore by the negative memories. I hope and I have prayed that this book will help you boldly move further into your purpose and that you will be able to enjoy your life as God originally intended for all mankind.

I have heard it said that by simply reading a book, you can gain the knowledge that took the author a lifetime to learn. That is why it is important to read and learn from others who have already been where you want to go. For example, if I want to learn how to be good in sales, then I may look for a book written by a very successful salesman. So it is that things can change for the better in a very short amount of time if you will apply yourself to learn. Proper treatment with accurate knowledge can cure a lifetime of pain.

If you want to increase in any area of your life, you must make the small changes in the direction you want to go. It is true that most mountains are moved a rock at a time and that mighty ships are turned by small adjustments. It's going to take some work to consistently go against what you feel like doing, but as you make the moves in the right direction, God will bring the harvest you're after in due season.

The information in this book is more than two decades of learning to do things God's way. It is possible to know God and still not listen to Him. It is completely up to you to listen and follow His instructions; He won't force you. There are many secrets for your life in the Bible, but only you can decide to pick it up and begin to study. Many bad things can be avoided and good things obtained when you take the time to read and then do what the Bible says. If you read and study over it, you will find the information you need. It's like when you buy a new car and the manufacturer puts the owner's manual in the glove box. If you take it out and follow it, your car will typically last much longer and require less repair because you have properly maintained your automobile according to the instructions of the one who created it. If you never open the glove box or if you discard the instructions completely, it will surely cost you more than you want to pay and possibly more than you can afford.

Another door opener to tormenting emotions can be disappointment. You may say something like this: "I am disappointed with my life. I really thought things would turn out differently." You may feel run down and exhausted; maybe you have even been diagnosed with chronic fatigue, anxiety, or severe depression. Disappointment may allow resentment to creep into your life without you even realizing it. You may even be angry at yourself; false guilt slips in saying that you could have or that you should have done something different.

One mental disorder that comes from extended emotional trauma is called post-traumatic stress disorder (PTSD).

PTSD may also include resentment, bitterness, and unforgiveness; it did in my case. I have discovered and believe that a big step towards the healing of many mental-health problems begins with forgiveness. You may simply need to forgive yourself or others involved in the cause of your PTSD. I am very familiar with PTSD because I was diagnosed with and have personally suffered from it.

When you're in a traumatic situation that it is completely out of control, it often seems there is nothing you can do to stop it. Sometimes traumatic events can haunt you for a lifetime, and you must reach for help if you want to be free. Asking for help is not weakness; in fact, it takes courage to allow another person into those areas of your life that you might even be ashamed of. I was not comfortable talking about it in front of others because sometimes I couldn't keep from crying, and I was embarrassed to cry. You might think, *if I would have done this . . .* or *if they would have done that . . ., then it wouldn't have happened.* Regardless of what you did or didn't do, it happened, and now you are left to deal with those haunting memories. But you are not left alone. You must forgive yourself and anyone else involved, if you desire healing. I learned this firsthand. I will share more about this in the following pages in a true story about myself as an army medic and a baby on this side of the Euphrates in Iraq.

It is extremely unhealthy to lock bad memories away and never speak about them, although many do. You may be one of them. Sometimes in life, bad things happen, and there is no answer or at least no answer that will satisfy. Many of us men have been taught that crying is weakness and that real men don't show their emotions. I have some news for you; if you didn't already know it, Jesus wept. God gave us tear ducts for a reason, but many times our pride holds us back from the release we need. I pray you will consider from this day forward that if you're truly interested in getting better, you won't resist crying when you feel the urge to do so.

We were not built for death; we were built for life and life more abundantly. When we encounter trauma that involves death, it goes against our innermost being, and that is why people cry at funerals. Good mental health is vital to a good life, and if you keep those emotions bound up in your mind, they will eventually come out. Most of the time, they come out in anger toward the people you love, and you say something and then regret it. When you have seen violent and horrific acts committed against mankind, it sears your mind, and it doesn't just magically go away.

You have to ask for help—help from God and from people. God has always used men and women to help other men and women. So don't be surprised if after you pray and ask God for help, certain doors open for counseling and such. Don't reject the help just because it doesn't come exactly like you expect it.

Prayerfully consider, and do the research. You were created to live and not die, so get to living and make choices that open doors of healing into your life. Don't allow the past to continue to rob you of your future for another moment.

*Please note: This book is not intended to replace professional treatment with licensed counselors and physicians. It is my hope and intent that it will be a tool that helps you in your journey to better mental and even physical health. I do believe that it is possible to recover from all sickness and disease, but I do not promote the idea of discarding your medications without confirmation from your physician. Your doctor will confirm God's work in your mind and body. In short, take your meds! I do know what it is like to suffer with severe depression and chronic severe pain. I can tell you that if you will decide to take steps toward God and His way of doing things, your circumstances will at the very least improve. I personally have chosen to trust God and to also trust the process that I believe will continue to bring full recovery.

Now I am going to share that story with you that I mentioned earlier. This is a true story about an experience that I had as an army medic in the desert of Iraq. This true story took place during Desert Storm, also called the Gulf War. I call this story "A Baby and a Medic on This Side of the Euphrates."

After receiving our orders to deploy to the Middle East, my unit was airlifted out of Fort Bragg, North Carolina, to an airfield somewhere in Saudi Arabia. President George H. W. Bush announced that we were drawing a line in the sand. We trained and trained in that desert for nearly six months before receiving our orders to advance into Iraq. Our unit was one of many coalition forces assembled to drive Saddam Hussein's military forces out of Kuwait. We charged across enemy lines after sunset on the eve of my twenty-second birthday.

I was serving my country with an elite group of doctors and medics assigned to the Eighty-second Airborne Division. I had been in the army for only sixteen months, and now I was in the Middle East in the middle of a war. After our commander confirmed that we were at our assigned coordinates along the Euphrates, he gave the order to set up, and we immediately assembled our Advanced Trauma Life-Saving (ATLS) unit. A brief description of our ATLS unit follows: There was a general-purpose (GP) large tent full of medical equipment, similar to an emergency room at your local hospital. It was equipped with four ER tables, two ICUs, and a lab. Tents were set up for X-rays and dental, and there were also two GP large tents used as recovery wards. Of course, all were fully staffed with soldiers operating them. My job was medic in the ER.

Soon we began taking heavy casualties, but the casualties weren't soldiers, as expected. In fact, they were mostly Iraqi civilians, including women and children. We had trained countless hours for this moment, but I wasn't expecting all these civilians. It was organized chaos for the next week or so.

Iraqi civilians were encouraged to rise up against Saddam Hussein, and they were called freedom fighters, but the problem was, most of these freedom fighters were unarmed! Saddam ordered his hired guns to attack these local civilians known as freedom fighters. So now there we were, army medics and doctors giving life-saving treatment to Iraqi civilians. You could see the fear and the desperation in their eyes as we worked hard day and night to help many of them live. I can remember one of the women yelling something in Arabic because she was in a panic, while some of the others were unconscious as we rushed to help them. We treated hundreds of civilian casualties in that first week alone.

I was on shift in the ATLS tent when I heard another ambulance roll up to the entrance of the tent. I rushed out to triage the arriving casualties according to protocol, but when the ambulance doors swung open, I had to look twice as my eyes focused. There lay a tiny baby in the middle of that long stretcher. This was the most traumatic experience for me, even though I had seen a lot already. We had helped many live, though some died, but what was a baby doing in the middle of this chaos? Immediately I rushed back inside the tent to find a bed, but they were all full except for one in ICU that our lab tech was using to do the daily blood count. Without much thought, running on instinct and adrenaline, I ran over and snatched that stretcher, consequently scattering his equipment all over the floor. All that was on my mind was helping that baby. There was no time to be cordial. Even thinking about it now, as those emotions race through my mind, tears are running down my face.

We raced to save that baby girl's life. First we established an airway, and then an IV was successfully started in her femoral artery. It is not easy to start a line on a baby, as an infant's arteries are tiny. Soon, with her vital signs stable, she was ready for transport to the navy vessel waiting in the Gulf (these ships are equipped with state-of-the-art technology that she would need for further treatment and recovery). As we were carrying her out to the Blackhawk for evacuation, I was gently holding her little hand. The moment we passed her to the evacuation crew, she squeezed my finger! It was almost as though she were saying thanks.

Sometimes I wonder how that young lady is doing. I hope she is well. Maybe she is taking care of her own little baby, or maybe she is a doctor or nurse. I am thankful that I was assigned to that team, that day, along the Euphrates, and helped save her life. There's nothing more satisfying to a medic than to save someone's life, especially an innocent baby's.

As soon as possible, I wrote home. I told my parents that I now knew why I was over there so far from home. At the time, I wasn't serving the Lord with my whole heart, but I did have a Bible with me. I remembered the Lord from when I was young. One evening I was at my truck, well after midnight, watching the sky glow red in the distance. I think it was fire burning from the fighting earlier that day, or maybe it was the oil wells burning. I reached for my Bible, and with my red-lensed flashlight, this is what I read: "Be strong and of a good courage, fear not, nor be afraid of them: for the Lord thy God, he it is that doth go with thee; he will not fail thee, nor forsake thee" (Deut. 31:6).

Years later I began to realize the impact those traumatic days had on my life. I was glad I was there to help, but inwardly I became very angry and bitter toward the person I believed who had caused all that suffering. I knew who had ordered the attack on those civilians, and I also now realized that the little girl probably was an orphan because of it. It is easy to rationalize that you have the right to hold a grudge, but forgiveness isn't about what's rational. It is about putting that person in God's hands and releasing yourself from the hold they have on you.

After returning home from Iraq and marrying my beautiful wife, we began to attend church regularly. I became an usher soon after, and one evening I was driving my pastor home from a Bible study in which the topic had been forgiveness. As we were driving home, somehow we began talking about the Gulf War. I remember him asking me if I had ever forgiven Saddam Hussein. Instantly I became angry and blurted out some bad words, including that my opinion was that he didn't deserve forgiveness. It became very quiet in the van, and I was angry and a little embarrassed that I had talked like that, especially in front of my pastor. It was then that I realized the anger and rage that was in my heart, because it spoke right out of my mouth. I was quickly learning a lot about the Bible, and although this forgiveness stuff was new to me, I knew in my heart what I needed to do if I was going to continue to follow Jesus.

I was at the church one afternoon praying, and this subject of forgiveness had been swirling in my mind for days now. So I began to pray something like this: "Lord, I don't understand why I should forgive such a man as this, but because it is in your word and you have forgiven me for all the bad things I have done, I forgive Saddam Hussein." Then suddenly it was as if a combat-loaded rucksack was instantly snatched from my shoulders. My knees literally buckled as that weight was removed! He took that burden just like He said He would.

I have learned that our Lord Jesus won't automatically take our burdens — we must give them to Him. It doesn't make sense in the natural mind to forgive someone who has done so much evil, but in the spirit realm, it makes perfect sense, because unless we forgive, we won't be able to receive God's forgiveness. "Judge not, and ye shall not be judged. Condemn not, and ye shall not be condemned. Forgive, and ye will be forgiven" (Luke 6:37).

One night I had a dream, and in the dream I saw an arm that had a bandage on it. As I continued to watch, a hand appeared and removed the bandage. The wound was coagulated and seemed to be healing well, but then the hand gently touched the scab with its index finger, and the scab just slid back very easily, uncovering a badly infected wound. The wound that appeared to be healing well was actually badly infected.

In the health-care industry, avoiding infection is taken very seriously. If infection gets into a person's bloodstream, he or she may go into septic shock, which can result in death unless it's treated quickly and aggressively with strong medications. At times we choose to hide our pain with a fake smile, but all the while we're dying on the inside as the infection of unforgiveness, bitterness, and resentment is coursing through our soul. Sometimes it just takes someone saying a certain word to reopen the wound, and just like in my dream when the finger gently touched the scab and revealed the infection that needed to be removed, that word exposes the anger or depression so that it can be removed.

Did you know that your spirit can be wounded? You are a spirit being living in a physical body with a mind and emotions that control your life. Harsh words cut and maim, and though we can't control what others say, I believe that we can learn to live above the pain if we are willing to cooperate with God. Choosing to quickly forgive or simply refusing to take offense is like a small key that opens the vaults of continual peace and joy in your life. It's a choice to soar above the storm or to go through it.

A couple of decades ago, I had the opportunity to literally see what it is like to fly above a violent storm. I was with a group of servicemen who were flying overseas, and the captain invited some of us to take a look out of his cockpit windshield just as we were flying directly over a lightning storm. It was an amazing sight to look down at all that turbulence and lightning, all while we were smoothly flying just above the storm.

I have learned and discovered that it is possible to rise above many of the storms in life. You can't do it alone, but when you decide to stay close to God by seeking Him in reading the Bible and in prayer, then you begin to understand how to stay above all the turbulence instead of stumbling or fighting your way through it every time. We all have storms in life, but I believe that we can avoid a lot of them by operating in the wisdom of God.

I believe we live on a planet that is governed by certain unseen laws. Of course, gravity is the most widely known, but there are a few more. For example, you may hear someone say something like, "What comes around goes around." Some people call it karma, but actually it is the law of sowing and reaping that's in the Bible. Here's one of the many references to this biblical truth: "Be not deceived; God is not mocked: for whatsoever a man soweth, that shall he also reap. For he that soweth to his flesh shall of the flesh reap corruption; but he that soweth to the Spirit shall of the Spirit reap life everlasting. And let us not be weary in well doing: for in due season we shall reap, if we faint not" (Gal. 6:7–9).

Have you ever said something critical about someone and then later found yourself doing the same stupid thing? Here's the warning: "Judge not, that ye be not judged. For with what judgment ye judge, ye shall be judged: and with what measure ye mete, it shall be measured to you again" (Matt. 7:1–2). Similar to gravity, you don't have to believe it in order for the law to work. I believe these laws are in our habitat because of the grace of God. Like someone said, you can do this the easy way or the hard way—you choose.

Certain patterns or ways of doing things are molded into us as we are growing up. I believe that the majority of our emotional responses have to do with what you and I were taught; we learned it from words and actions. I want you to seriously think about this next statement. I am completely and fully persuaded that each of us imagines God the Father is a lot like our earthly father. I believe that we subconsciously expect the same reaction or nonreaction that we grew accustomed to in our childhood. If our father was mean, we think God is mean; if our father was passive, we think God is passive. If your father was gentle, loving, and kind with great compassion and patience, then you're in good shape. If not, you need to learn and understand the truth about Father God, if you haven't already.

Have you been physically, mentally, or sexually abused? Maybe it was from the people who were given charge of your protection, but instead violated you. In your life, you have many decisions to make, and I hope that today you will decide to forgive those who have hurt you. If you choose to cooperate with God, He will remove the pain and heal the wounds. It may take some time for some wounds to heal, as some are more serious than others, but if you will simply decide to daily walk in forgiveness, the results will be wonderful! Decide that you will be a forgiving person every day of your life, and then when you're tempted to hold a grudge, it will be easier because you've already made your decision.

I used to believe that you could just suck it up and drive on, no matter what happened, but I have learned that sometimes you need to stop and receive inner healing before you continue forward in life's journey. I have also learned that God will not force you to forgive. He will nudge you in the right direction, but you must respond to His prompting to see results. God has healing in His hands. Won't you take His hand today? Simply pray, "Thank You, Father, for sending Jesus to suffer and die for me.

I do believe that He is exactly who He said He is and that He rose from death on the third day just like He said. I repent today, Lord Jesus, and I thank You for saving me. You are now my Lord and Savior. Amen."

This book was written for you, and it isn't a coincidence that you are reading it at this particular moment in your life. The information in this book will be a blessing to you and to others in your life. Now I am going to share a story with you relating to the importance of treating every wound. Although fictitious, this story could easily be something that has happened.

It was just after sunrise when the next ambulance rolled up to our ATLS facility with more wounded. My first patient was an adult male U.S. soldier, and upon initial exam, I discovered three injuries. First and most obvious was the sunken chest wound. After inserting a chest tube and applying proper bandaging, I moved on to the next life-threatening injury, which was an open wound on his right shoulder. After removing shrapnel and then suturing the wound, I began to evaluate the last small injury. It seemed minor, a small cut approximately five inches above the left knee, I simply cleaned and bandaged it, applying a small bit of bacitracin ointment to the two-by-two-inch gauze bandage. With the IV administered on slow drip, along with the proper antibiotic, the patient was taken to one of our wards so that he could rest and heal.

Soon the attending nurse was making his rounds and discovered the patient nonresponsive. Cyanosis had set in, and my patient had died! What seemed like an insignificant cut above the left knee was actually the entrance wound from a piece of shrapnel from a grenade. That small sharp piece of shrapnel had traveled through the layers of skin and muscle, finally lodging in the femoral artery. If you're familiar with that type of injury, you know that it is possible to hemorrhage to death without losing a single drop of blood outside the body.

Think about it like this: Like that small piece of shrapnel, words can hit you much harder and cause greater damage than you first realized. Words can cut you to the core, especially negative words that are spoken by someone you respect and love. Inwardly you are hemorrhaging profusely and don't even know it. You feel empty and numb, but you can't seem to put your finger on the cause. Unforgiveness may be the cause of those types of symptoms.

I believe that it is vital to speak to someone about even the seemingly small wounds in your life; that small thing may be what's draining the life from you. Talk to God, go into your room and shut the door, turn off the phone and television, and stop all distractions. Take time to contemplate your life before your creator so that you may be healed. It is also important to talk to a human. Speak with someone who has some answers and someone you know you can trust and who wants you to be happy.

I believe that the Lord doesn't want you and I overwhelmed. I believe He works with us in a gentle and kind process. Only He knows exactly what you know about yourself and those negative issues of life that you have been through or may currently be in. Precious metals have contaminants in them, and they require a certain exact amount of heat to remove the dross and make those metals perfectly pure. It is also true that diamonds and other precious stones are developed under extreme amounts of pressure over long periods of time. Pressure may be used to push bad things out of your life, if you cooperate with God. It may be something locked deep in your soul, in the vaults of your mind, that you have knowingly or subconsciously pushed down and refuse to think about. Only you have the power to choose what you will do with the information in this book. No one, including God, will force you to forgive. It is a choice of your free will to forgive or to continue to drink that tormenting cocktail.

I am purposefully mentioning possible negative events that may have caused you pain throughout this book, but please recognize that if your injury isn't mentioned specifically, the same precepts and decisions will open the door for healing regardless of the cause of the wound. Keep in mind that treating injuries may initially cause a bit of pain, as when you're splinting a fracture or injecting numbing medication when prepping a wound for sutures. Although bad memories are painful, just remember that it is the doorway to healing that wound once and for all.

Maybe your first love was a bad experience; you loved them, but they rejected you. Maybe someone that you trusted with all your heart betrayed you. You took vows planning to spend the rest of your life with that person, but they decided to leave when things got tough. Perhaps someone close to you died, and you go over in your mind that if you had done things differently, they wouldn't have died. Maybe you lost a child, and you blame yourself for not being there or think you could have done something different. That is when you must forgive yourself. Life is full of the unknown, and many times things just don't make sense. Holding yourself hostage will only hurt you and the people you love. Perhaps the promotion you worked so hard to obtain was unjustly given to another person. The list is endless of the ways you may have been offended and hurt. We all have many opportunities in our lives either to hold a grudge or to quickly forgive. It is up to each of us to make the best choice, and I pray that by the time you finish this book, you will be fully persuaded that forgiveness with much mercy and grace is always the correct and best choice.

These offenses build up over long periods of time, and they work against you in your subconscious. Then someone says something and it irritates you, but you're not sure why. You catch a glimpse of someone and immediately have negative feelings towards them because they look like someone who caused you pain in your past. The sound of a voice or certain phrases may set you on edge. You have these triggers but have not yet connected the dots as to why.

Maybe your father or mother talked down to you, saying things like, "You'll never amount to anything. You're stupid, and you'll never amount to anything." Or maybe they made sarcastic comments like, "You really make me proud" when you did something bad or just made a mistake. So often parents say things that were said to them when they were children without realizing the possible harm it will do to their children that they dearly love. It is possible to do and say foolish things without realizing what you've done.

Remember when Jesus was telling His disciples how He would have to suffer and die, and Peter rose up and said, "Not so, Master"? Then Jesus rebuked Peter, saying, "Get behind me, Satan!" (Matthew 16:22–23). Jesus was rebuking the influence that was speaking through Peter. Can you imagine walking and talking with Jesus, watching Him perform mighty miracles, and then have Jesus tell you that He was going to be handed over to evil men and be beaten and crucified? I am certain it would cause fear, and when that fear came, it would open the door for evil to speak.

I believe it's the same today. Think about the times you have said things that you wish you wouldn't have said and then asked yourself, *what was I afraid of?* Be honest. Many times when parents say wrong things to their children, it is motivated by fear of the future. Parents want their children to do well, but sometimes they say some pretty stupid things trying to motivate them. It is important to understand such things because it makes it a little easier to forgive people when you see their motives were pure. Peter just didn't want to see His Lord have to suffer, just like none of us want to see our loved ones suffer.

They beat Jesus till His eyes were swollen shut and then mocked Him, saying, "Now prophesy to us who hit you" as they took turns punching Him with fists of rage and hatred. They made a crown of thorns and shoved it on His head, mockingly calling Him the king of the Jews. They beat Him with a scourge until Jesus was unrecognizable and then nailed Him to a cross and crucified Him. After all of that, "then said Jesus, Father, forgive them; for they know not what they do. And they parted his raiment, and cast lots" (Luke 23:34).

That was not just something Jesus said to be nice. They really didn't know what they were doing, and it is the same today in many situations when people are mean to us. They really don't know the pain they are causing. Of course, that isn't always the situation, but it is something to consider. I hope you will consider the idea that the people or person who harmed you may have been influenced by outside forces. The Bible says, "For we wrestle not against flesh and blood, but against principalities, against powers, against the rulers of the darkness of this world, against spiritual wickedness in high places" (Eph. 6:12). The truth is, you and I have an enemy who wants to cause us harm, but God keeps us from harm when we stay close to Him. Jesus said, "The thief cometh not, but for to steal, and to kill, and to destroy: I am come that they might have life, and that they might have it more abundantly" (John 10:10).

Did you know that the Bible teaches us that God sometimes speaks to us in dreams? "And it shall come to pass afterward, that I will pour out my spirit upon all flesh; and your sons and your daughters shall prophesy, your old men shall dream dreams, your young men shall see visions" (Joel 2:28). I was having a conversation with a man that I have known for many years when he told me about a dream or vision that he had (he wasn't sure which). After some days of others fasting and praying for him, he began to see himself when he was a child; and at two certain ages, he saw what looked like a shadowy dark figure that had entered his life. Trauma opens the door for bad influences to enter our lives, but with accurate diagnosis and good ministry, those influences can be driven out of our lives. I believe the Lord showed my friend that vision or dream so that he could connect the dots of the negative events that had influenced his life so that he could forgive and be set free and healed.

The Bible calls those bad influences "tormentors," and the only way they leave is when we invite God to remove them from our lives as we cooperate with Him. Forgiveness is a very powerful tool in the spirit realm of life, and if we learn to forgive quickly, we will reap the spiritual benefits that only God Almighty can distribute. I am not sharing these truths to scare you, but so that you will see how the enemy tries to harm you. You see, the enemy is the one who constantly attempts to bombard us with fear, but God doesn't operate like that. In fact, here is what the Bible says about fear: "For God hath not given us the spirit of fear; but of power, and of love, and of a sound mind" (2 Tim.

1:7). Many times the Bible says, "Fear not." The Spirit of Jesus leads us with peace; He doesn't drive us with fear.

If you have received Jesus as your Lord and Savior, then you have authority over all the power of the enemy. In fact, God has placed you in the seat of authority with Jesus: "And hath raised us up together, and made us sit together in heavenly places in Christ Jesus" (Eph. 2:6). So, you see, you have absolutely no reason to fear the enemy, because God gave you *His* authority. When you learn to rest in the Lord, fear will have no effect on you. You will simply sit where God has seated you and will rest in Him, knowing that you can trust Him.

With the discovery of DNA, we now know that we are each a specific creation designed and built for a specific purpose that we alone can accomplish. There's no one exactly the same as you. God knows you because He created you, and He has the hairs on your head numbered. God alone is the only other person who knows everything about you, besides you. Relationship with God is the easiest relationship you will ever have. He knows why you do what you do and say what you say. He has been watching over you before you came out of the womb. Regardless of what you have done, He still loves you, and because of that love, He has made an escape from the wrath to come through His one and only Son, Jesus.

The Bible, God's laws and His wise instructions, is always for our good. He is a loving Father who wants only good for His children, but just like children, we have to choose to listen and follow His instructions or to rebel and pay the price that rebellion costs. Just like laws are put in place by governing authorities for our protection and justice on the earth, God has established laws for our protection. These laws or instructions are in the Bible, and it is our responsibility to read and understand God's way of doing things on the earth. Living according to the Bible is the good life. Peace and joy follow the life that chooses to follow God.

Jesus said that He came to bring good news, to let us know that through Him we can be free in every area of our lives. Here is exactly what Jesus said: "The Spirit of the Lord is upon me, because he hath anointed me to preach the gospel to the poor; he hath sent me to heal the brokenhearted, to preach deliverance to the captives, and recovering of sight to the blind, to set at liberty them that are bruised, to preach the acceptable year of the Lord" (Luke 4:18–19; Isa. 61:1–2). Jesus wants to heal us everywhere we hurt, but you and I must choose to cooperate with Him. We cooperate with Him by following His instructions, which include forgiving those who have hurt us.

God isn't pleased with those who have harmed us, but remember, it is also very likely that we have wounded someone ourselves. We are all God's creation, made in His image, but unlike God, we are not perfect. At some point in our lives, we have caused pain for someone else. Listen to this verse from the Bible: "All we like sheep have gone astray; we have turned everyone to his own way; and the Lord hath laid on him the iniquity of us all" (Isa. 53:6). We all have fallen short in some way or another, and we all need God's grace and mercy.

When God created Adam and Eve, the Bible says that He placed them in the Garden of Eden. Eden translates as a place of pleasure, so, you see, it was God's intent that we live in pleasure, not pain. Sin crept into that garden in the form of a serpent, and when Eve ate that fruit and Adam followed suit, mankind was introduced to evil. Now the Lord did not leave us in that fallen state, because He sent His Son so that we might be put in right standing with God once again.

Simply by faith in God's plan of salvation through Jesus, we are made new.

"For I will be merciful to their unrighteousness, and their sins and their iniquities will I remember no more"(Heb. 8:12). God isn't up in heaven just waiting for us to mess up so He can strike us down or disapprove of our actions. He is patiently waiting for you and me to choose to cooperate with Him and say, "Lord, I ask you to search my heart and make me clean in your sight. Father, I thank you for sending Your Son to take the burden of my sin, and just as you forgive me, I choose to forgive those who have caused me pain."

Maybe you have been reading this book but have been thinking, *I will not forgive them. If you knew what they did to me, you wouldn't forgive them either.* I know that men and women do some awful things to each other on the earth, but it is your decision to either hold on to the bitterness or to let it go and let God heal you. It is an act of faith to obey God and step in the direction of forgiveness. If you will mean business with God, then He will mean business with you. If you do something halfheartedly, don't expect much in the way of results; but if you are seriously ready for a change, then God will back His Word.

I want to emphasize to you that when you choose to forgive, you are not saying that the evil done to you was just. You are saying that you are now placing it into God's hands and trusting your life to His way of doing things. Forgiveness opens the doors for healing and miracles in your life. In the final pages of this book, I am going to share many scriptures with you that confirm that what I'm writing is sound, biblically based doctrine. Just like the engineer who designed and built a certain bridge or building knows every detail about it, so does the God who created you know every detail about you. God has a plan for your life, and it is better than you have imagined.

You may have not expected anything good in your life. In fact, I have learned over the years that many people expect only bad things, and when something good happens, that is abnormal. I would have to write another book—and I just may—to further explain this topic, but for now, here is what the Bible says: "For

I know the thoughts that I think toward you, saith the Lord, thoughts of peace, and not of evil, to give you an expected end" (Jer. 29:11).

In the army, soldiers are taught to follow their last direct order. At times this doesn't seem to make sense, but the commanders of the battlefield have intelligence from higher sources, such as satellite imagery and drones, that gather information from investigative work done before and during the conflict. As soldiers, we followed our last direct order in combat while resting in the knowledge that our commanders saw the battlefield from a higher advantage.

God has seen your future, and He has information that can keep you from harm if you will simply trust Him. God sees the ambush ahead, and He will keep you from walking into it if you will listen. Not only does He see the ambush, but He knows how to keep you on the path of a successful life. Here's scripture about that: "Trust in the Lord with all thine heart; and lean not unto thine own understanding. In all thy ways acknowledge him, and he shall direct thy paths"(Prov. 3:5–6). So, you see, it is simply your job to trust and acknowledge, and it is His to direct your path.

I believe the Bible is perfect information given to us in this life that at times can be like a war. The Lord has given us the perfect plan in a book called the Bible. All we have to do is study it, learn it, and do it, and it will always bring us into a good place. Here's what the Bible says about the Bible: "All scripture is given by inspiration of God, and is profitable for doctrine, for reproof, for correction, for instruction in righteousness"(2 Tim. 3:16). You and I can rest in knowing that our commander God has given us good and reliable information, and we can follow His plan in the Bible for success in our journey here on the earth.

I hope and I have prayed that you will consider what I am sharing in this book and that you will act upon it. Remember, your creator originally placed man and woman in a garden of pleasure with intentions of a good life. Only after their rebellion did the hard times begin. It is the Lord's will for us to start each day with childlike expectation, waiting to see what good things will happen that day!

When we learn to walk in God's kingdom that Jesus established on the earth, we now know that He wants us to live in peace and joy. "For the kingdom of God is not meat and drink; but righteousness, and peace, and joy in the Holy Ghost" (Rom. 14:17). Learning to operate in God's kingdom on the earth may seem foolish to those who do not know Him. Jesus tells us, "But I say unto you, Love your enemies, bless them that curse you, do good to them that hate you, and pray for them which despitefully use you, and persecute you "(Matt. 5:44). This seems unfair, if we don't understand that it is for our good, and that we operate by faith, believing God's Word is always for our good. So what may seem foolish to many is really the wisdom of God.

Here is a scripture to confirm it: "But God hath chosen the foolish things of the world to confound the wise; and God hath chosen the weak things of the world to confound the things which are mighty" (1 Cor. 1:27).

We know that following God's instructions may seem foolish, but if we don't follow the teachings of Christ, then this is what the Bible says: "And every one that heareth these sayings of mine, and doeth them not, shall be likened unto a foolish man, which built his house upon the sand: And the rain descended, and the floods came, and the winds blew, and beat upon that house; and it fell: and great was the fall of it" (Matt. 7:26–27). The house represents our lives, and the rains and floods and wind represent when life gets very difficult. Jesus said if we don't do what He teaches, then destruction is inevitable; but when we listen and do what He says, our lives will be able to withstand the mighty storms of life.

The most important thing to understand is that Jesus came to give you a new blood covenant of salvation in His holy name, Jesus. The enemy wants to harm you, but Jesus came to heal you and keep you from harm. "The thief cometh not, but for to steal, and to kill, and to destroy: I am come that they might have life, and that they might have it more abundantly" (John 10:10). Another verse says it another way: "For this purpose the Son of God was manifested, that he might destroy the works of the devil"(1 John 3:8). You and I must be aware that we have an enemy, and we must also be aware that Jesus has already defeated him.

Jesus wants us to be slow to anger and quick to forgive because it is for our benefit to do so. You see, the Scriptures show us that when we refuse to forgive, we are turned over to the tormentors. Here is the story that Jesus told, confirming what I have written:

> Then came Peter to him, and said, Lord, how oft shall my brother sin against me, and I forgive him? till seven times? Jesus saith unto him, I say not unto thee, until seven times: but, until seventy times seven. Therefore is the kingdom of heaven likened unto a certain king, which would take account of his

servants. And when he had begun to reckon, one was brought unto him, which owed him ten thousand talents. But forasmuch as he had not to pay, his lord commanded him to be sold, and his wife, and children, and all that he had, and payment to be made. The servant therefore fell down, and worshipped him, saying, Lord, have patience with me, and I will pay thee all. Then the lord of that servant was moved with compassion, and loosed him, and forgave him the debt. But the same servant went out, and found one of his fellow servants, which owed him an hundred pence: and he laid hands on him, and took him by the throat, saying, Pay me that thou owest. And his fellow servant fell down at his feet, and besought him, saying, Have patience with me, and I will pay thee all. And he would not: but went and cast him into prison, till he should pay the debt. So when his fellow servants saw what was done, they were very sorry, and came and told unto their lord all that was done. Then his lord, after that he had called him, said unto him, O thou wicked servant, I forgave thee all that debt, because thou desiredst me: Shouldest not thou also have had compassion on thy fellow servant, even as I had pity on thee? And his lord was wroth, and delivered him to the tormentors, till he should

pay all that was due unto him. So likewise shall my heavenly Father do also unto you, if ye from your hearts forgive not everyone his brother their trespasses.
—Matthew 18:21–35

Christians are like the first servant, who simply by asking was forgiven of his debts. Now what right do we have to hold anything against anyone, knowing that Jesus, the perfect Son of God, has forgiven us? Now I'm going to ask you to make peace with God if you have not already. Please go somewhere quiet where you won't be interrupted at this holy time between you and God. Also grab a piece of paper and something to write with, as you will need it, because I want you to take a few moments to write down names, and anything else you want to write down, describing who and what you have been reminded about while you were reading this book. Write it down on a piece of paper that you can discard, because like Jesus did for you, you are going to cancel the debts of those who have harmed you. After praying over them, you will then discard those names as an act of forgiveness.

Back to the issue of making peace with God if you haven't already. The best way to explain receiving Jesus' forgiveness is from the Bible, so here is what it says: "That if thou shalt confess with thy mouth the Lord Jesus, and shalt believe in thine heart that God hath raised him from the dead, thou shalt be saved. For with the heart man believeth unto righteousness; and with the mouth confession is made unto salvation" (Rom. 10:9–10).

Pray this and mean business with God: "Father God, I ask you to forgive me. I receive Jesus, and I confess Him as my Lord and Savior. I believe you came to earth as God in the flesh, born of the Virgin Mary. You were falsely accused, and then you were crucified and buried, but You rose on the third day! You did all of that for me, Jesus. Thank You for saving my soul, Lord Jesus. Amen." (Now you're born again. You're made new in the sight of God Almighty and have a clean slate, a fresh start!)

Now take that paper with the names or initials and hold it in your right hand. Hold it up to God, and pray this: "Father

God, I thank you that you have made me righteous by the blood that Your Son Jesus shed for me. Now, Lord, just as you have forgiven me, I forgive these people [say the name or names out loud] now. Lord, I release them. They owe me nothing. I have forgiven their debts just as you forgave mine. Now, Lord, I ask you to release me from the torment that was set against me for my rebellion to Your Word. I command all torment to leave my life and never return, in the name of Jesus! Thank You, Lord Jesus, for setting me free!" Who the Son sets free is free indeed! Now rip that paper up and throw it away as an outward sign of your inward decision to forgive.

My prayer for you is this: "Father God, I thank you for the work you have done in my life, and especially for the work you have done this very day for my brother or sister. Lord Jesus, I thank you for making yourself so very real to my friends as they take the time to seek you. Father, I ask that you would always remind us to make the correct decision when we are tempted not to forgive. Lord, I thank you for the new beginning you have given us. In Jesus' holy and mighty name, I pray. Amen.

I have provided some blank lined pages at the end of this book. I hope that you will use them in your journey of forgiveness. Perhaps you will want to write a letter to God about what you have read, or maybe you want to write something about this subject of learning to forgive. You may want to write a letter of forgiveness to someone who has already passed away or maybe to someone that you are unable to speak to face-to-face at this time.

Letters of Forgiveness

Stop The Torment!

Stop The Torment!

Stop The Torment!

Stop The Torment!

Stop The Torment!

Stop The Torment!